MW00878530

Peter's Pointers

LOVE YOUR EGO

as you love your Self

PETER MARCHAND

LOVE YOUR EGO as you love your Self

Copyright © 2019 Peter Marchand

Published by Peter Marchand
Jeroom Duquesnoylaan 8,
9051 Sint-Denijs Westrem – Belgium.
www.leela-yoga.org

Cover illustration by Tatjana Smet
see www.sundalini.com

Peter's Pointers n°1

Peter's Pointers is a series of booklets aimed at giving a brief but direct overview on a particular subject. For people who like to know more, reference is given to other sources of information, such as the many online classes freely available on www.youtube.com/youyoga.

INTRODUCTION

Over the past year, videocalls have enabled me to do more individual yoga coaching of people that have been enjoying my online classes. I was surprised to find that many of them are still having a rather negative attitude towards their Ego. Somehow my teachings fail at communicating the obvious : we are all very lovable and without accepting and loving ourselves as we are, progress is impossible.

Likewise there hardly exists any book on the divine nature of our dear Ego in yoga philosophy. For many self-help books it is a central theme, yet these lack the depth of understanding provided by yogic insight. So I would like to make the issue perfectly clear by looking at our Ego from all angles provided by ancient yogic scripture. I hope it can make the reader more at peace with themselves and not blocked in moving forward, which seems to be happening all too often.

Yoga and meditation are supposed to make us happier, not less happy. At the beginning, it does so for most people, but after a while the experience may sour. People are naturally impatient, while some are definitely perfectionists in everything and likewise in their spiritual practices. That is not wrong, but wrong understanding can turn it into a powerful obstacle.

People involved with yoga these days want to be so much like a yogi, live only in the now, have no desires, let go of unhappiness, walk the talk, be that divine Self, destroy their Ego... Expectations are a root cause of unhappiness. The desire for enlightenment is also a desire. It can make us very unhappy if our expectations are not reality based.

A little unhappiness may cause one to be more sincere in the practice. Yet fundamental dissatisfaction with our Ego will not lead to deeper practice and will definitely not bring us peace. It will reduce our confidence, stop progress and lead to depression, delusion and emotional blockage.

If we can look at length in the mirror without feeling unhappy, we can walk the highest yogic paths. I hope this book can provide such a mirror. For a while it may be hard to accept our Ego as it is. Yet, I sincerely wish that the reader will come to love this child as I do and enjoy the divine beauty of its lotus blossom unfolding.

Peter Marchand

CONTENTS

ACKNOWLEDGMENTS

Gratitude to the miracle of life always comes first. I also feel so thankful to all my teachers, who guided and inspired me on the path of life.

I especially thank the following beautiful people for their honest comments on the draft version of this book : Alexia De Wandeleer, Dave Goodings, Dong Zhang, Nadia Tavajjoh, Neta Katz, Rebecca Daldini, Santosh Prasad, Stephanie Rees Squibb and Will Geraets.

Gratefulness is also due to the following editors for the great selfless service of finetuning the language : Karen Hamdon, Margo Hay-Goodings and Régine Deruyver.

More than gratitude is due to my life partner Tatjana for her loving support, so many inspiring interactions on the contents of this book also, and of course for the unique feat of synthesizing the entire book in just one image, her artful cover illustration.

Grateful and somewhat dazzled I humbly accept Swami Asokananda's heartfelt endorsement, which can be found on the back cover.

———

1
THE SELF & OUR EGO

The Self is the pure conscious energy which is the center of every being. When we stop thinking, we exist and we know that we exist : that is the Self. In essence it is unmanifested potential. It clearly exists in us, but it has no form. In that way we can say it is empty, though it is filled with pure being. The Self never changes, because only what has form can change. As a result of being changeless, the Self has no desire and is ever in bliss. That makes it the key objective of yoga, as it allows us to be happy whatever happens.

The Self is experienced as the conscious feeling of "I am". The Ego is the thought of "I am that". We feel "Oh I am" and then we ask "But what am I ?", which we answer with "I am that". So the Self and the Ego are very much related, as both are based on the same "I am". The only problem of the Ego is a small misunderstanding about "that". When the Ego says 'I am that", it limits itself. Because of the dividing nature of our mind, it seems to say "I am only that".

So, the "I" searches for existence within the form, while in essence it is formless and in fact, it can take any form. That is the basic misunderstanding of the Ego and yet, the Ego also has some relative truth. Compared to the absolute truth of the Self, the truth of the Ego is temporary. Yet, it means that in every moment the truth of the Ego also has an absolute quality, one step in a holy dance. Everything happens only once upon a time. The Ego is at the same time an illusion[1], as it is the divine actor[2] in the theatre of life[3].

One might picture the Ego as the king of the country which is the body, while mind is the country's administration and the Self is God. The Ego is a natural attribute of our manifested existence within a form. Just like our stomach, hands and feet, the Ego has a function. Somebody has to take charge of our body, otherwise, how could we even lift a hand ? In fact, we have many bodies, called the sheaths of

---

[1] "Maya" in Sanskrit, the power or smoke that hides reality - see youtube.com/youyoga "Jnana – Layers of Consciousness (Koskas)"

[2] "Radhe" in Hinduism is often seen as the divine form of the Ego, beloved of Krishna as the Self – see youtube.com/youyoga "Divine Energies of Hinduism"

[3] "Leela" in Sanskrit – the divine play or theater of life, see youtube.com/youyoga "Jnana – The Truth"

consciousness[4], in which the Ego has a role to play. In addition to the physical body, there is the energy body, the body of conscious thoughts, the body of the subconscious mind and the body of the Self. One might picture these sheaths as concentric veils that hide the light of the Self at the center, with the physical body as the outermost layer.

---

[4] "Koshas" in Sanskrit – see youtube.com/youyoga "Jnana – Layers of Consciousness (Koskas)"

2

THE PHYSICAL BODY

Traditionally speaking, the Ego is the one who identifies with the physical body[5]. Then "that" is the body, which is made of the food we eat[6]. It consists of the five elements earth, water, fire, air and space[7], of which the entire universe is also made. When the body is threatened, the Ego feels insecure. If we think we might be seriously ill for example, it is not so easy to let that fear go.

It is in relation to the physical body that we can most easily see how natural the Ego is. How could we survive without at least some identification ? What

---

[5] "Ahamkara" in Sanskrit, which means "I am the flesh" – see youtube.com/youyoga "Jnana – Layers of Consciousness (Koskas)"

[6] "Annamayi Kosha" in Sanskrit – the illusion (maya) of the sheath (kosha) of food (anna) – see youtube.com/youyoga "Jnana – Layers of Consciousness (Koskas)".

[7] "Tattvas" in Sanskrit, corresponding to solids, liquids, gasses, fire and space – see youtube.com/youyoga "Jnana – Layers of Consciousness (Koskas)"

would happen if we say "Oh this body is hungry, but that is not my problem as I am not the body". It would be totally unnatural, even if in truth we can never die, because we are not the body. Without some attachment to the body, the game of life cannot be played.

The Ego is the caretaker of the body, so at least that much identification is needed for this body to survive. Not only all having the same Self makes us one. We all have a belly too. Sure, some saints survive without food or water, but that is because they know other ways to give the body what it needs. Using breath or whatever technique, they still care.

In as far as we value our feelings, taking care of our body goes well beyond feeding it. We are advised to keep it pure as a temple, inside and outside. Both happy and unhappy emotions leave biochemical and energetic residues in our tissues and organs. They produce healing as well as disease. Through these residues the body also increases our emotional inertia, the tendency to stick to a certain emotion for some time. Physical exercise, natural rejuvenating remedies as well as healthy foods assure that our emotional feedback loop with the body is uplifting rather than bringing or keeping our mood down.

3

THE ENERGY BODY

Apart from the physical body made of matter, which is also energy, we have our more subtle bodies, which are purely made out of energy. In the vital energy body[8] that holds the life force and is fed by our breathing, we experience emotions like love and anger, courage and fear, joy or sadness, etc.

The energy body can be active or passive, or neither active nor passive[9]. In the active state we feel like doing things and might just as easily engage in laughter as in anger. When our energy is passive, we might need rest or activity, depending on whether our tiredness logically follows a more active period or on the contrary, has become more of a habit. In both cases, feelings of sadness, fear and depression may

---

[8] "Pranamayi Kosha" in Sanskrit – the illusion (maya) of the sheath (kosha) of vital energy (prana), see youtube.com/youyoga "Jnana – Layers of Consciousness (Koskas)".

[9] "The "Gunas" "Rajas, Tamas & Sattva" in Sanskrit – the essential qualities of energy, see youtube.com/youyoga "Yoga & Ayurveda".

increase. When our energy is neither passive nor active, we are peaceful, happy and enjoy more subtle emotions and activities. Yoga and meditation generally increase this gently energy, while breath is our main tool in mastering our energy body.

The Ego also identifies with our emotions. Instead of saying "I am feeling angry" it often makes the mistake of saying "I am angry". So, the "that" then becomes the anger. If we feel we are the energy of anger, then how can we ever get rid of it ? This is a misunderstanding, because the anger is just a temporary feeling. Our true, everlasting yet often hidden, deepest feeling is one of bliss.

It is equally a misunderstanding to think "Oh my energy body is feeling some anger, but that is not my problem, because I am the pure Self, in which anger does not exist". Then we can't deal with whatever is causing the anger to dominate our energy. Being in charge of the quality of our energy is a main objective in yoga. Our feelings are messengers that intuitively attract our attention towards something that actually needs our attention. Not getting caught by the energy of anger solves many minor irritations, which can be rather misplaced anyhow. More serious anger however requires us to get involved.

7

Real anger, fear, disgust or sadness come from within, from our even more subtle subconscious mind. We will not be able to simply let them go. If we try to ignore them, we merely suppress them. They will keep boiling inside, which is very unhealthy. They will stop us from truly feeling happy, no matter what Buddha smile we put on our faces. Suppressed emotions will disturb any attempt at deep meditation[10] or increase the effort needed to reach that state.

---

[10] "Samadhi" in Sanskrit, see youtube.com/youyoga "Samadhi".

4

THE CONSCIOUS MIND

The next body is the mental body, the body of thoughts[11]. Here another identification takes place, when we believe to be this thinking. Then we think that these thoughts are ours. When we learn to observe our thoughts, we can see how they are mostly random associations. They appear as objects of our observation, just like the objects of the senses that we can hear, see, smell, touch or taste. They are not who we are.

Thoughts belong to the natural, automated function of our mind, which is to interpret the many bits of data that come in through our senses. Mind has to rapidly determine which data are important through this process of semi-random association. Our thoughts also regulate our incredible ability to send

---

[11] "Manomayi Kosha" in Sanskrit – the illusion (maya) of the sheath (kosha) of mind (manas), see youtube.com/youyoga "Jnana – Layers of Consciousness (Koskas)".

9

many bits of data to our body to allow it to walk, jump, handle objects, write and all these things that we do. So our mind is a very busy administrator, that has to jump from here to there like a monkey. This does not mean that we have to do the same.

The one who truly identifies with all the thoughts that come to his mind must declare himself a lunatic, a schizophrenic, a neurotic. How many contradictory thoughts do we have ? How crazy is our thinking ? Sometimes we may think we want to hit someone. If we believe that these thoughts are truly the expression of what we want, it can be quite dangerous. The truth is that sometimes we want to hit someone and sometimes we want to kiss them. So what to make of our thoughts, changing all the time ? It is surely best not to identify too much with what comes to our mind.

Another limitation of mind is the dividing tendency to think in terms of opposites. We mostly think hot or cold, hard or soft, loud or silent, far or near, big or small, good or bad, etc. Yet, when we want to use mind for philosophy, we have to replace this "or" of opposites by the beautiful "and" of complementaries. Then we can see that the truth is in pleasure and pain, in good and bad luck, in student and teacher, in body and mind, in Ego and Self. Mind is programmed to separate one experience from another and we have to be wary of this tendency whenever we draw conclusions on the meaning of life and everything. The ultimate truth is unity in diversity, which is the kind of concept that mind cannot really comprehend. It goes well beyond the world of names and forms, which is the universe of mind.

Likewise, our very popular reasoning faculty has a limited capability to answer the bigger questions in life. Reasoning is a chain of linear thinking that jumps from one detail to the next. The value of our conclusion usually depends on the premise we started from, which is not necessarily based on fact or reason. If that premise is wrong or only part of the truth, the entire conclusion is useless. Reasoning can be very useful in a practical sense, but it easily makes us lose sight of the whole picture. Whatever happens in life is the result of a complex interaction between different forces, so the value of the usual cause-and-effect thinking process is quite limited.

Yet again, if a thought is persistent, then to ignore it completely is not a workable idea, unless you want to meditate of course. Just as our feelings are messengers, our thoughts are pointers that teach us something. Thoughts offer very practical ideas and help to understand the relationships between the things that we observe. They also point to certain desires, fears, tears and frustrations, that are present in our subconscious mind, which is an even deeper level of our being. However we may try to ignore them, if the thoughts persist they will continue to do so, until we do something about it. If we don't, they will just spin out of control, becoming more obsessive.

The natural task of the Ego in the conscious mind is to keep our thoughts more or less balanced. It is no easy task, as the two-edged sword of our thinking can prove any thought to be right. The Ego is often in doubt as to which thoughts to believe. The conscious mind can only provide the question, yet for the correct answer the Ego has to look deeper. In order to be able to do that, regular meditation is actually required. Habitual thought suppression, which is meditation, generally keeps the noise down in the conscious mind even when thinking. This way the inner voice of the subconscious mind can be heard more clearly whenever it speaks.

5

THE SUBCONSCIOUS MIND

Even more subtle than our conscious mind is the subconscious mind, also called the intellect or the body of concepts[12]. While we can say it is like an encyclopedia of knowledge, ideas and memories, it is not an encyclopedia that we can read just like that. It is beyond our conscious thought.

The subconscious mind does not only consist of ideas and memories, but also contains our karmic imprints[13] from this and past lives. That involves very deep personal feelings, the origin of which may be long forgotten. They determine our more instinctive reactions. It's like a body full of subtle, yet powerful energetic vibrations, a great galaxy with many star systems. It carries our deepest desires, our essential

---

[12] "Vijnanamayi Kosha" in Sanskrit – the illusion (maya) of the sheath (kosha) of knowledge (jnana), see youtube.com/youyoga "Jnana – Layers of Consciousness (Koskas)"

[13] "Vasanas" in Sanskrit – that which remains, see youtube.com/youyoga "Reincarnation, Karma & Dharma."

fears and frustrations, as well as our deeper attachments. It also contains impersonal information from the cosmic intellect[14]. This pure knowing manifests as true intuition and also in deep meditation, when cosmic secrets are revealed through it.

In ancient scripture four modes of speech[15] are described, or four phases through which speech develops. First, there emerges a subconscious, wordless feeling. Secondly, the feeling is translated as one or a few words coming to our mind, appearing on the interface between the subconscious and the conscious. Third, the words are converted into a conscious thought, an actual sentence. Fourth, we might speak our thoughts out loud or not. Of course, the process is not as linear as described here. Anytime during the second, third and fourth stages, new feelings respond from deep within. They echo our thoughts, again and again affecting our conscious thinking. Funny enough for those who can see and appreciate the joke, the most essential source of our most serious thoughts is wordless, instinctive, subconscious. Everything we think, say or feel originates

---

[14] "Buddhi" in Sanskrit – origin also of the word "Buddha".

[15] "Vak" in Sanskrit – see youtube.com/youyoga "Speech fasting".

beyond our consciousness, even as the conscious mind also adds to it through reasoning and association.

The subconscious mind is the primary seat of our Ego. It is not just in our conscious thoughts that we identify with the physical body or any of the other bodies. Much more powerful is the subconscious attachment to these bodies, various aspects of the "I am that" which are buried deep inside of us. So, if we tell ourselves that we are not these bodies, then this primordial, subconscious Ego does not so easily agree.

Conscious thinking can affect the subconscious mind for sure, but only a little. According to western science, the conscious mind is mostly related to the frontal brain, while the subconscious mind relates to the mid-brain, the hind-brain and the brain stem, the reptile brain. Science confirms that to a small degree the frontal brain can affect the other parts of the brain. However, if our reptile brain feels that the body is threatened or that our person is disrespected, it may lash out like a cobra. Conscious thoughts will not have the time to interfere.

Our subconscious mind not only carries memories, feelings and desires from this life, but also from past lives. With the Self at the center of it, the subconscious mind is the individual soul[16] that travels from this life to the next. So it also contains the desires for which we were born in this life. Maybe we like to be a musician, desire to be wealthy or want to meet somebody. These are the primary karmic forces that brought us into this life and into this body. They reside in our soul and cannot easily be ignored or reasoned away.

Suppose that one primarily was born in this life to be with a person that one has loved in a past life, which happens to many people. And suppose that unfortunately in this life one cannot have a love relationship with that person, because they already have a love relationship with someone else. Then we can tell ourselves a hundred times that this person is nobody special, that there are plenty of fish in the sea. In the end it will not make much of a difference. Unless enlightenment is near, our whole life we will desire to be with this person. If that is not possible we may accept it on the surface, but if the smallest opportunity for togetherness manifests then again that desire will emerge.

---

[16] "Jiva" in Sanskrit – see youtube.com/youyoga "Karma, Dharma and Reincarnation".

Some people have a strong desire for wealth, because they were very poor in their last life. Some will be very afraid of water, because in their past life they drowned. Some people will have a strong desire for sex, because they prematurely chose to be celibate monks in their past life or maybe ended up in a sexless marriage. Some may want to be somebody important and respected in society, because in their subconscious mind they remember the experience of being downtrodden. Many will have the strong desire to be in a nice love relationship, because truly for most people in most lives, such true love does not come easily. In the same way, some will desperately want kids, a guitar, spiritual knowledge or the peace of meditation in a cave. To ignore these desires goes against our very soul, against the purpose of this life, against the very energy of creation. So, if you desire to withdraw from life to find something, rather than escaping from something, then please do. If not, then don't.

Imagine that a person reduces his list of desires and attachments from say 100 to just 10 over a certain period of time. It is well known that such a person will find that the 10 remaining desires and attachments will have a strong tendency to become much more powerful. Renunciates usually have very few possessions, depending on the rules of the spiritual organization to which they belong. With rather many one may experience how they become overly attached to the few possessions they have left. This shows how our desires and attachments are only symptomatic of our deeper subconscious urge to attach.

This reflects the seemingly endless grasping of the Ego for things to hold onto. The Ego is full of existential fear and thus seeks to prove its existence and importance. The true Ego is not only the Big Ego that most people associate with the word Ego. It is also the Little Ego, the frightened inner child. It knows very well how vulnerable our body is, how fleeting any nice feelings or relationships can be, how easily forgotten are our wisest thoughts. The issue of desires and attachments is not the actual issue. The true challenge in yoga is to make the Ego - residing in the subconscious mind - trust and relax, as a snake relaxes to the music of the snake charmer. Then desires and attachments will naturally become less powerful, ready to be fulfilled or released.

When observing our physical body, energy body or thought-body, the conclusion is basically that the Ego should identify with each just enough, but not too much. When it comes to the subconscious mind however, the conclusion cannot be the same, as we have no conscious control over the subconscious. Only in as far as these subconscious impulses lead to conscious thoughts and feelings, we can get some idea of their existence and try to deal with them in the best possible way. Then we can see for example how our past relationship to our father affects our current relationship to our partner. This is where self-study becomes an unraveling of the personal self, the Ego, rather than the discovery of the universal Self. This is where we realize that our subconscious primal fear, and all urges related to it, take time to evolve and heal.

It is important to mention the existence of the spiritual dimension, which lies beyond the world of the five elements and senses. The energies there can strongly trigger the karmic impressions in our subconscious mind, through the medium of the cosmic mind field. This means that some of our hidden emotions or desires may become powerful stumbling blocks. They may require some kind of subtle energy healing before we can evolve further. It also means that the spiritual world can be quite instrumental in resolving subconscious blockages.

If there is one reason why the Ego does not simply disappear with the proverbial finger snap, it is because of the subconscious mind. Yet we can learn to be happy whatever happens, even if what happens goes against our innermost desires, fears and frustrations. That is where the different paths of yoga can help us, gradually but surely dissolving our attachments and connecting us more and more to the Self.

6
THE SELF

Our innermost core is the Self, consisting of pure conscious energy[17]. The pure consciousness and the pure energy are two sides of the same coin, two aspects of the one Self. The "individual" inner Self is not in any way different from the Cosmic Self. The Self has no size, so size doesn't matter to it. Similarly, looking at a drop of water through a microscope, it is no different from the ocean. Having no form, the Self cannot change, so there is nothing to desire or be unhappy about. Contrary to our other energy bodies, the quality of this most subtle energy body thus never changes. It always remains in bliss, which is the greatest blessing of the universe.

It is only the Ego who can actually think "I am that Self". When fully residing in the Self in deep

---

[17] "Anandamayi Kosha" in Sanskrit – the illusion (maya) of the sheath (kosha) of bliss (ananda), see youtube.com/youyoga "Jnana – Layers of Consciousness (Koskas)".

meditation[18], we are beyond thought and beyond even the pre-thought vibrations of the subconscious mind. In the Self, pure conscious energy is a fact, not a thought.

Although what truly happens in deep meditation remains a mystery beyond words, we might say that the Ego has then merged with cosmic consciousness. At least, it appears to be absent in that state and whether it then still exists or not is a matter of semantics. It was actually never truly separate from the Self. In any case, the temporary merging with the Self leaves a strong imprint on the Ego afterwards. It will have acquired the memory of its true nature.

This temporary merging does not destroy the Ego. The subconscious mind may still hold on to its old complex patterns of desires, fears, etc. To entirely remove these karmic imprints, more is needed than just one really deep meditation. The process towards true enlightenment is said to take many lifetimes for a reason.

As all thoughts somehow relate to it, the Ego is the very first idea in the subconscious mind. The Ego takes precedence over all other ideas, even the idea of the Self or enlightenment. The Ego is the Self, as it

---

[18] "Samadhi" in Sanskrit, see youtube.com/youyoga "Samadhi".

manifests in the form. It's will, based on its desires, rules whatever happens. The Self has nothing to decide, while the Ego has the holy kingly duty to decide. To sense where happiness lies in each moment and chose accordingly. To live life.

All that truly matters is how wise king Ego rules, in choosing which desires to fulfill and how to do it. It can be rather confusing. What makes us happy ? The inexperienced Ego will go for shiny things. The wise one will seek happiness in simple things and in the heart. That one intimately knows the value of our heart connection, the ability to consciously witness the universe through the Self. Whatever disturbs this connection is not desirable, meaning anything that goes against the law of love & harmony which is the law of the Self[19]. As the Self is one in all, love is evident. Whatever strengthens this connection is desirable at any moment. All else can be desired and enjoyed at will. To live life.

Connecting to the Self is the best answer to every question, yet it is still the Ego who has to decide to make the connection. When connected to the heart of the Self, we connect to everything else as well as to ourselves. Loving others unconditionally is impossible

---

[19] "Dharma" in Sanskrit – see youtube.com/youyoga "Yoga Dharma".

without   loving oneself. In the Ego, trust in oneself slowly has to replace the fear of being somehow not worthy or lovable.

7
SEVEN STEPS TO ENLIGHTENMENT

Ancient Vedic scripture describes how the process that leads towards enlightenment and the complete disappearance of the personal Ego consists of seven logical steps or phases[20]. They are steps, because each brings us closer to the goal and lifts the energy upwards. They are phases as they each require some time to become fruitful. Our spiritual evolution requires to dance up and down this stairway quite a lot, all the while gradually moving up.

The first step in this ancient thought system starts with the desire to be happy whatever happens. Usually because we tire of our unhappiness or of the unhappiness that we perceive in the world, we get the idea to escape the game of like and dislike, happiness and unhappiness. It's a very daring idea, the first step on a beautiful journey, yet only the beginning.

---

[20] "Bhumikas" in Sanskrit, see the Varaha Upanishads and also youtube.com/youyoga "7 Steps to Enlightenment".

.

The second step leads us to study and Self-study[21], revealing the different yogic paths and the blockages upon these paths. We become students of happiness, of the main source of unhappiness which is the Ego and of the main source of happiness which is the Self.

The third step comes when we put the theory into practice and start meditating earnestly. It is here that all techniques and disciplines of yoga are used to finally obtain the direct but temporary experience of the Self in deep meditation. To reach this goal requires at least a temporary forceful detachment from all other desires[22]. This third step is crucial to any true progress, with many people getting stuck for a long time in thinking about yoga rather than doing it.

In the fourth step, we have sufficient experience of the Self through deep meditation. Thus we are sufficiently identified with the Self, even when we are not meditating. This phase is called Self-realization by Ramana[23], who distinguishes it clearly from actual enlightenment, even though many people confuse these two. It means that we can actually be happy

---

[21] "Vichara" in Sanskrit – holding still, see youtube.com/youyoga "Jnana Yoga Technique".

[22] "Vayraga" in Sanskrit, see youtube.com/youyoga "Detached Attachment".

[23] Ramana Maharishi is probably the most famous Jnani teacher of the 20th century.

whenever we want[24], because we have the ability to instantly reconnect to the Self, if and when we want. The karmic impressions in the subconscious mind cause us to sometimes set aside this power, allowing unhappiness to reveal our hidden desires, fears and frustrations. It is a lengthy process in which all our remaining karmic desires are fulfilled. It will take as much time as desires remain written on our inner bucket list. This fourth stage can be reached by anybody in this life, which cannot be said for the following stages. It depends on how many lives we will need to fulfill our remaining desires. Here we try to achieve our goals without creating any new karmic debts, maintaining harmony with everything else. Yet it still happens somehow that we overstep ourselves and act without respect to others. Then a keen loss of contact with the heart, with the Self, is experienced as unhappiness, which rapidly brings us back on the love track.

In the fifth step, we have become entirely without desire and totally unattached to anything but the Self. There is no longer any forceful detachment, just natural, true non-attachment. What remains to be

---

[24] "Sattvapatti" in Sanskrit – ruler of the subtle energy (sattva), see youtube.com/youyoga "7 Steps to Enlightenment".

done is the full payment of our karmic debts, through specific actions in selfless service. If we already have been quite helpful to others in the earlier phases, we can more quickly clear our karmic account.

In the sixth step, no debts are left and we stop perceiving the outside world, having no more interest there.

After a while, this naturally leads to the seventh and last step of enlightenment or liberation, where the sense of individuality is entirely lost and only pure cosmic conscious energy remains.

Since we tend to move up and down this stairway to heaven quite a lot, one might say that even when we have reached the fourth stage we still need to apply the techniques of yoga. However, from the fifth stage onward, everything happens naturally instead of forcefully. It is in the third and fourth stages that regular practice is essential and correct perception of the nature of our Ego and our desires is crucial.

8

GOING IN AND OUT

The basic process of yoga is most clearly synthesized as the in-going and out-going paths[25]. The in-going path of yoga is primarily the path of meditation, leading to the temporary merging with the Self. The out-going path of yoga is where we learn to keep the bliss and peace of the Self, even when not meditating. Here we aim at manifesting the Self in life. In all yoga practice we regularly shift between concentration and relaxation, between going in and coming out.

While the in-going path logically precedes the out-going path, both are complementary parts of the process of yoga. We meditate, find something, come out of our meditation and try to hold on to that thing. As long as our peace and bliss rapidly disappears

---

[25] The ingoing path is known as the path of Shiva, while the outgoing path is named the path of Vishnu, see youtube.com/youyoga "The Union of all Yoga's".

when we open our eyes, we have gained very little.

To dive deeply is a requirement for success in bringing out the feeling of the Self in life. To remain sufficiently in peace and bliss while acting out our roles in life, is just as important in order to give our next meditation the chance of going even deeper. All too often meditation practices do not achieve much more than compensation for the stress and unhappiness experienced in life.

The in-going path is associated with the ascetic yogi, who forcefully withdraws from life and detaches from all desires, except the one desire to reach the Self. This detachment can happen one hour a day, one day a week, one month in a year or even for many years. However, it is no use to withdraw to a cave if all one does is dream of the world outside. And neither is it a good idea to stay in the world if we always dream of the peace of the cave. Which of these two paths gets the most attention during a certain period of time depends on our desires and on our karmic duties.

Fully withdrawing from life for a lifetime as a renunciate is a relatively new phenomenon, only about 1300 years old[26] in the Hindu tradition, while in Buddhism monks existed already during the life of Gautama Buddha[27]. In the Vedic tradition, life was divided into four logical phases[28] : pure learning as a youth, raising a family as an adult, gradually passing on the household responsibilities to the younger generation as one gets older and withdrawing from the world as a renunciate towards the end of the life. Already near the end of the first phase, the ability to have a temporary experience of the Self was supposed to be gained. To withdraw from life for a while was advisable during any phase, but generally not considered as a lifetime commitment.

The saints and seers[29] of more ancient times, who are the source of the original Vedic knowledge, were known to have wives or husbands, children and a job. They lived as householder yogi's in full temptation and confrontation with the rewards and struggles of life. That also allowed them to fulfill their deepest desires

---

[26] "Sadhu" or "Sanyasi" in Sanskrit, a tradition generally seen to be formally installed by sage Adi Shankara in the 7th Century, see youtube.com/youyoga "The Union of all Yoga's".

[27] The founder of Buddhism, who lived in the 4th and 5th Century BC.

[28] "Ashramas" in Sanskrit : "Brahmachari", "Grihasti", "Vanaprasta" and "Sanyasi" see youtube.com/youyoga "The Union of all Yoga's".

[29] "Rishis" in Sanskrit, see youtube.com/youyoga "The Union of all Yoga's".

in a harmonious fashion, the out-going path. Likewise, their students were living at the house of the teacher[30], helping in the household. Both meditation and life were used to bring them closer to the Self.

To see the ideal yogi exclusively as someone who is completely withdrawn from life - almost as a life sentence - is incorrect. Renunciates have been known to come out of their caves after decades of meditation and still experience some very natural desires to be there. For the one who is entirely beyond desire, it does not matter whether he lives in a cave or in the world. To be a monk yogi or a householder yogi is a personal choice, with neither being superior over the other.

All yogis must somehow or other follow the five universal, complementary yogic paths :

• In the yoga of meditation[31] we gradually learn to meditate, to stop thinking, so that the Ego is no longer continually fed by thoughts, allowing the Self to come forward in deep meditation.

• In the yoga of right knowing[32], our thinking is

---

[30] "Gurukul" in Sanskrit, see youtube.com/youyoga "The Union of all Yoga's".

[31] "Ashtanga Yoga" in Sanskrit, the yoga of eight limbs - also known as Raja Yoga or Patanjali Yoga, see youtube.com/youyoga "The Union of all Yoga's".

[32] "Jnana Yoga" in Sanskrit, the yoga of knowledge or truth, see "The Yoga of Truth", Peter Marchand, Destiny Books 2007, ISBN-13 978-1-59477-165-1.

fully focused on the Self, reducing the Ego by truthful reasoning and by moving our attention beyond the thoughts towards the one who is observing the thoughts.

- In the yoga of love[33] our feelings are focused on love of the Self in each and every thing, so that the Ego is reduced by purification of our emotions and by strengthening our heart connection to the universe.

- In the yoga of selfless service[34], our actions become a sacrifice to the Self and the universe, reducing our Ego through purification of our actions and the resulting reactions[35].

- In the yoga of transforming the energy[36], support from the spiritual world is improved, directing healing energies towards all our bodies including the subconscious mind, so that our Ego is reduced by unblocking our energy channels and innermost desires.

---

[33] "Bhakti Yoga" in Sanskrit, the yoga of spiritual devotion and love, see youtube.com/youyoga "Bhakti Yoga : the Yoga of Love and Devotion".

[34] "Karma Yoga" in Sanskrit, the yoga of pure action in selfless service, see youtube.com/youyoga "Karma Yoga & Yoga Teaching".

[35] "Karma" in Sanskrit means action or reaction, which is also destiny, as Karma is most often understood, see youtube.com/youyoga "Reincarnation, Karma & Dharma".

[36] "Tantra Yoga" in Sanskrit, the yoga of magical energy, see youtube.com/youyoga "Tantra in Bhakti Yoga".

Thus the 5 main yogic paths deal with all that we can do in life. We can think, feel, act, try to do nothing or try to do all these four at once, which is the working principle of any transformative magic[37]. These five practices exist for thinking correctly, for feeling connected, for acting in harmony, for doing nothing and for transforming our energy.

The yoga of meditation makes all other yoga's possible. And it requires many preparatory practices, including postures, breathing, sense withdrawal, and concentration[38]. It also involves temporary withdrawal from certain disturbing actions in life, as well as maximally focusing on activities that promote our inner peace[39]. When concentration in meditation is stable, the meditator can leave the scene and the screen of knowledge becomes clear[40].

The resulting deep meditation will help to resolve

---

[37] The "magic" of "Tantra Yoga" means the ability to change some energy inside us or around us by means which are incomprehensible to the mind, yet are nevertheless true and not fake, see youtube.com/youyoga "Tantra in Bhakti Yoga".

[38] "Asana, Pranayama, Pratyahara & Dharana" in Sanskrit are four of the limbs of Ashtanga Yoga, see various classes on "Ashtanga Yoga" at youtube.com/youyoga.

[39] "Yama & Niyama" in Sanskrit are the first two limbs of Ashtanga Yoga, see various classes on "Ashtanga Yoga" at youtube.com/youyoga.

[40] "Dhyana & Samadhi" in Sanskrit are the last two limbs of Ashtanga Yoga, see youtube.com/youyoga "Samadhi".

the issues in the subconscious mind, by looking at them from the neutral Self, rather than from our conscious mind. As a result, the subconscious mind becomes more relaxed on these issues. This relaxation allows us to practice letting them go in life. Like a person who always has been quite shy, may lose that quality in deep meditation, yet still will have to manifest that in life before the transformation is completed.

It is the combination of all main yoga techniques that leads us towards the temporary merging of the Ego with the Self. Thus the objective of phase three upon the path towards enlightenment is attained. It is also this combination that allows us to fulfill our principal desires in a harmonious way and thereby realizing the objective of phase four of the path.

9

PRINCIPAL DESIRES

The upward movement of energy through the chakras[41] represents an evolution of our desires towards higher levels. It is a natural process by which desires are exhausted through fulfillment. It is the main creative drive behind the universe. These principal desires originate in the elements earth, water, fire, air and space, our gross and less gross energies. Desires are activated by the passage of the life force through these elementary energy centers, causing the Ego to identify with them.

The first chakra is located at the base of the spine and originates with the earth element or solid matter. It produces attachment to the form of the physical body, seeking to secure it. This attachment first occurred when the soul entered the miraculous new

---

[41] "Chakras" can be translated as wheels of energy or energy centers, but since it cannot be properly translated, it is better to use the original term, see youtube.com/youyoga "The Desires of the 7 Chakras".

unit of matter known as the fetus. It brings the desire for financial security for example, which can be fulfilled by having a regular job and income. Some people of course may become addicted to greedily acquiring more and more wealth. That however shows a blockage in the energy of that chakra, not the normal natural process of a healthy personality.

When people feel relatively secure through their work, desire naturally evolves towards having some fun, the second chakra desire. This chakra is located in the genital area and is water-based. It produces attachment to the liquids in our body, where emotions are experienced as subtle chemicals called neurotransmitters[42]. Here the emotional enjoyment of the senses and the fantasies of our mind get all our attention. Yet, after a while, too much partying becomes boring.

Thus the desire is born to achieve something, to be somebody important, which is the third chakra desire. This navel chakra is fire-based, producing attachment to what is seen in the light, such as the achievements of others or our public image. Then one can work hard

---

[42] Known as the physical aspect of the "Rasas" or essential emotional energies, the juice of emotion that is found in the blood plasma, see "The Yoga of the Nine Emotions" by Peter Marchand, ISBN 1-59477-094-8 - and also many Rasa classes on youtube.com/youyoga..

to obtain a respected position in society. It usually produces envious competition and not all that much happiness.

Experiencing the emptiness of outward achievement, the fourth chakra desire develops to actually be loved instead of only being respected. This heart chakra originates in the wind element, which produces attachment to others who breathe the same air and life force as we do. It manifests as the longing to connect to a partner, to have a loving family life, to belong to a community or to be at one with nature and the universe. Such love however has the downside that we no longer only suffer from our own problems. The pain and suffering of our loved ones also become our pain and suffering.

Thus the fifth chakra desire for more understanding is born, hoping to better protect our community, also by teaching them how to avoid suffering. This throat chakra desire originates in the element of space or ether, which produces attachment to understanding by broadening our horizon and taking a distance. We want to find out why problems in life keep coming, even though everybody seems to try hard to have a good life. We start looking for a more fundamental solution and study psychology, sociology, philosophy, health and yoga.

After a significant amount of study we come to the conclusion that the solution is not in understanding, but in a different kind of being. Then we move from thinking to doing. We want to achieve the true aim of yoga, which is the merging of the Ego with the Self. So at some point, we want nothing less than enlightenment, the desire of the sixth chakra. This chakra is located in the third eye between the eyebrows and originates in the super element[43] that holds the source of all elements. It produces the desire to unify with the source of all being, which is the Self.

Then we seriously start to meditate and live like yogi's. The more we progress the more we may achieve the desireless state of the crown or seventh chakra, moving entirely beyond the elements.

Once we have reached the desire of the sixth chakra, our energy can freely move from the first to the sixth chakra. Yet it must be clear that as long as we still have desires in the chakras below the seventh, they will first require a solution before we can truly move up there. We will not be able to just meditate all that away. We need time for our desires to mature

---

[43] "Mahatattva" in Sanskrit, see youtube.com/youyoga "The Desires of the 7 Chakras".

through the chakras, which partially happens through their fulfillment.

The evolution of desires through the chakras towards higher levels is a natural process, which nobody can escape. In the end, everyone is predestined to become enlightened, in this life or another. So the question is not how to forcefully speed up the process. The challenge is how to avoid remaining attached to desires that we have already exhausted and are no longer satisfying.

10
EXHAUSTING DESIRES

Humans are not gods, who only give. Neither are we demons, who only take. We are human beings, who are meant to give and take. We do our work[44] and then we reap the fruit of our work in fulfilling our desires.

In economic law, it is said that things become more valuable the more they are scarce, and less valuable the more they are abundant. We want what we don't have or what is hard to get. What is readily available holds little attraction, because we already had it. Thus desires evolve by getting fulfilled. When a desire is really satisfied, it evolves towards more subtle yet higher levels of enjoyment. When a full closet of chocolate cookies holds no more attraction, our taste moves beyond, towards more healthy foods for

---

[44] "Karma" in Sanskrit – also meaning action or reaction, which is also destiny, as Karma is most often understood, see youtube.com/youyoga "Reincarnation, Karma & Dharma".

example.

Ancient scripture also describes in a very simple way four natural human desires[45]. The first desire is wealth, which generally speaking means to have what we need to live a good life. The second desire is for enjoyment of all kinds, and especially the enjoyment of the senses and mind. The third desire is for achieving harmony and has many aspects, such as harmony in a community, in a diet, in a garden, in a song, in the relationship between various desires, etc. The fourth human desire is enlightenment.

One is free to choose the particular importance given to each desire, depending also on duties and needs. This essential freedom might mean for example that a person spends 50% of the time at work, 25% in entertainment, 20 % in social work or the arts and maybe 5% in meditation. It is a good idea to think for ourselves what those percentages are and evaluate if they actually represent what we want.

We need to differentiate between needs and desires. Modern society offers many riches, but at the same time it is not easy to make ends meet. Yet we

---

[45] "Purusharthas" in Sanskrit - the wealth's of the soul, "Artha, Kama, Dharma & Moksha", see youtube.com/youyoga "Yoga & Bhoga (Enjoyment)".

may consider what percentage of our income, attention and time go to things we acquire but do not need.

While we are totally free to choose what desires are important to us, we are also free not to lose time and energy on desires that are not important to us. There is always something more waiting behind the bend in the road, something even more juicy. Mainstream culture and economy tend to just drag us along upon the same safe and straight paths that hold little adventure.

Harish Johari[46] used to say "If a desire comes to mind best ignore it, because mind easily comes up with all kinds of useless desires. If it comes again, continue to ignore it, as mind can be quite persistent. But if a desire comes to your mind again and again, then please go for it". While he warns against just running after every desire, he also encourages us to fulfill the deep desires for which we were born.

This advice follows the basic Tantric understanding that desires can be removed by fulfilment. Suppose one repeatedly experiences the

---

[46] Harish Johari authored many books, was a gifted painter and sculptor, a composer of Indian music and my first teacher since I was 20 years old – see also www.sanatansociety.org.

desire to appear in the press and on TV and become a well-known personality in the local community. Why not find a way and have the experience ? One may conclude that becoming well-known does not make one very much loved, so this third chakra desire may transform into the fourth chakra desire for true, unconditional love. Maybe one doesn't have to go through it to fully accept this also on the subconscious level, but then again maybe one does. When in doubt, feel free to try.

Exhausting our deepest desires by fulfilling them surely beats suppressing them. The more we suppress them, the stronger they become. Very often, that is how addictions are born. Suppose once upon a time, one felt like getting very drunk just to be able to forget some difficult passing phase. There may have been other ways to deal with it, but suppose one really felt that this was needed. If then for whatever reason one held back and only drank a little, it is not going to work. Then one will need that little bit of alcohol every day just to keep the negative feeling away a little. Before one knows it, one is addicted to it. When having decided to do something, don't hold back.

Obviously, this does not mean that we can just

pursue any desire regardless of the consequences to ourselves, our body and others. It is very advisable to fulfill a desire only when it does no harm. Wait for the right time, the right place, the unique opportunity that the universe will provide, and then go for it without restraint. The wise one knows there is a power called karma, the law of sowing and reaping. Sometimes the fulfillment of a particular desire will have to wait quite a while for the right circumstances, maybe even until our next life. Who cares ? There are plenty of desires for sure with which to fill this life. There is no need to stress about it. We have eternity at our disposal.

Desires are natural, they are an integral part of life. According to ancient Vedic scripture, they are the purpose and energy of creation[47]. This universe was not created for everybody to run away from. In creation, pure consciousness ever remains the same, while the energy ever changes, bringing many forms and experiences. Desire itself is the primary force behind these changes and manifestations, literally creating the power needed for its fulfillment. Next to the miracle of the one Self, there is the miraculous diversity of our multiple Ego's, virtually traveling

---

[47] In Sanskrit, the word "Shakti" does not only mean "goddess" or "energy", it is also translated as the "power, purpose, desire and energy of creation".

through time and space while manifesting our inner desires.

The ultimate joy of the universe is to be able to enjoy the illusion of it as a real game. We play it fully, but without getting lost in it. We know very well what is truth and what is not. Some games we win and some we lose, but we never lose our smile.

The only thing needed for having a healthy relationship with our desires is to replace the usual "I want this" by "I might want this". That means, if circumstances allow it, I will fulfill the desire, if not then I won't. While desires themselves cannot be morally judged, their fulfillment does require a heartfelt sense of right and wrong[48].

There is nothing wrong with desires as such, which leads us to the question why we so easily doubt this simple, natural truth. Why does the story of yoga seem to fundamentally question our desires ? Where does the idea come from that our Ego is something bad, that we need to get rid of it as soon as possible ?

---

[48] "Dharma" in Sanskrit – see youtube.com/youyoga "Yoga Dharma".

11

UNHAPPINESS

In sadness[49], the Ego feels the pain of separation from that to which it feels attached. In fear[50], the Ego anticipates the same pain. In anger[51], the Ego feels disrespected and treated unfairly when this pain seems to be caused by others. In depression[52], the Ego takes this pain the most personal, losing faith in the ability to avoid it.

Unhappiness is that pain that the Ego experiences when life forces us to let go of some attachments. This conclusion is not depending on whether the attachment is to what we have, to what we imagine to

---

[49] "Karuna" in Sanskrit - which also means compassion, see youtube.com/youyoga "The Joy of Suffering".

[50] "Bhayanak" in Sanskrit - which also includes anxiety and worrying, see youtube.com/youyoga "Fearlessness".

[51] "Raudra" in Sanskrit - which also includes more mild irritation, see youtube.com/youyoga "Stop getting angry".

[52] "Vibhatsya" in Sanskrit - which means disgust and is the essence of depression, see youtube.com/youyoga "Depression never again".

have or to what we would like to have. In the world of names and forms, nothing is permanent. Attachment may bring enjoyment for a while, yet all attachments naturally end in potentially painful, forced detachment.

Thus unhappiness is caused by our attachments, leading to the question why we so eagerly attach ? Behind every attachment, a deep uncertainty of our Ego is hiding. It is most clearly demonstrated by the great feeling that we get when somebody expresses their love of us. Then we may feel that maybe, just maybe, we are worthy of love, as if that isn't self-evident. Somehow, we all have low self-esteem, even if some have less than others. Narcissists that are so full of themselves are not loving themselves too much. They desperately seek to be loved, because in truth they hate themselves. They are like children fighting for attention.

The immense popularity of the negative view on the Ego and its attachments originates with this rather inherent low self-esteem. If some teachings confirm this feeling and blame ourselves, some will believe. If these teachings add to it the possibility of true escape, nothing less than total desireless bliss, more will believe. People very much like to believe that escape from their unhappy life and Ego is possible.

The Ego is the source of all unhappiness for sure, yet that does not mean we should ignore it, hate it, destroy it and make that our big life philosophy. The idea that we need a big solution starts from the idea that there is a big problem. And that is how most big problems are created. In truth there is not even a problem. The Ego and its desires can create big problems indeed, but in themselves they are no big deal. Only if we think they are, will they become huge.

The Ego is just as natural as our hands are. Both can be doing good or bad, hurting others or healing others. It only depends on how we manage them. Sure the terrible wars in the world are all products of the Ego, but to make war on the Ego is just going to make it worse. The Ego is an uncertain child. What kind of an adult do we get when a child gets told every day that it is bad, or an eternal loser, filled with sinful desires ?

Unhappiness is a bad adviser. Let us first embrace our inner happiness, then see what is true or false about our Ego. Ego-bashing in itself is a natural enough mistake, caused by misunderstanding and fueled with unhappiness. In different forms, it has been around for ages.

Yet meanwhile, what to do with this unhappiness ?

49

As long as we do not have the direct experience of the Self in deep meditation, it is not easy to love our Ego. The answer to that question goes totally beyond the scope of this book, yet it seems unfair not to answer it at all.

We are certainly advised to meditate as much as possible. Yet when unhappiness is strong, deep meditation is hard to achieve. The more we calm down our energy, the more the inner struggles resurface and disturb our focus. Until we can overcome this lack of concentration, we have to be patient. Our meditative practices calm the mind and relax the Ego, so unhappiness will also be reduced. Mantras that are more energized by seed sounds[53] can be particularly helpful. Too much expectation however blocks any deep meditation, because to gain this state the meditator has to disappear.

Meanwhile it also advisable to regularly remove excess tension from the body through physical exercise and breathing. Paying attention to the food we eat, as well as keeping our body clean and the living environment pleasing, is very helpful. Regular

---

[53] "Bija" in Sanskrit – these seed sounds are particularly effective to counter energetic disturbances from the subconscious mind and are especially used in Tantric mantras.

foot massage assures our connection to the earth, so that tension can naturally leave the body. This just to name one type of helpfull wellness that is no luxury, as we can easily do it to ourselves. Reducing addiction avoids excessive sensory input, which drains our vital energy. Definitely, we should also seek out the people and teachings that seem to improve our inner peace. Energy workers can be very effective, provided they know what they are doing.

If unhappiness seems to be all we have to work with, we may become students of its different flavors[54]. We can learn to reduce anger and irritations by questioning our expectations. We can remove the dissatisfaction with ourselves by building up discipline step-by-step. We can overcome fear and worrying by avoiding to imagine the future and living more in the present moment. We can share our tears through compassionate care for other beings, expanding our sadness towards all who are suffering. In togetherness, even suffering becomes more enjoyable.

As long as we are not non-attached, why not try to

---

[54] "Rasas" in Sanskrit - which means emotional essences and also essential emotions, see "The Yoga of the Nine Emotions" by Peter Marchand, ISBN 1-59477-094-8 and also many classes on youtube.com/youyoga.

attach more wisely ? Everything in the end has to go, yet many great things are quite permanent during the short length of our lives. Enjoy the sun, the stars, the rain, nature and the arts. Some ice-cream on the way is not that bad. We can try to focus on what we have and avoid too much thinking about what we don't have. With a little attention we can also try to be less attached to what we are attached to, and even practice detached attachment[55]. Ignore feelings of loneliness by loving all. If we feel powerless, why not build up strength ? Why not meet our ignorance with some heartfelt wisdom ?

If rose bushes do not get pruned regularly, they become weak and die. As the saying goes, what doesn't kill us makes us wiser, as we learn to appreciate every problem as an opportunity for spiritual growth. Few worthwhile things come easily. If nobody ever had a problem, then nobody would discover the bliss of meditation. The more we resist the forced detachments that are natural to life, the more painful they are. Whatever comes, must go. Accept that there is no life nor love without some sacrifice. We can try to open our heart as wide as we can and humbly surrender our life to the good cause

---

[55] See youtube.com/youyoga "Detached attachment".

of spiritual evolution.

In any case, refuse self-hate. We are a work in progress, so what is there to dislike ? Slowly but steadily, happiness will overcome. As long as a peek at the Self is all we get, keep peeking.

12
TAKING A PEEK

For Self-realization, we need to learn to stop the changes in our mind, to stop our thoughts. This way the Self, which is beyond the experience of mind, can come forward[56]. Stopping all thoughts is not easy, but definitely not impossible, even if quietening our thoughts may be where to start.

When meditation starts working, some bliss of the Self can be felt. It is here that we have to be very careful not to make the mistake of looking at the outside world and our Ego in disdain. If that happens, it means our experience of the Self just didn't go deep enough. It means our bliss is so weak that it feels threatened the moment we reenter the game of life.

One might say that in between the mind and the Self, there is a wall and one only has been peeking over that wall, catching only a glimpse of what lies

---

[56] Free translation of the basic definition of yoga from the "Yoga Sutras of Patanjali" 1.2, 1.3, 1.4.

beyond. But already the Ego is attached to the feeling of it. So we try to defend this fleeting feeling against the whole world and in doing so we may create a huge problem, which has nothing to do with the world.

When we truly find ourselves to be over the wall and have the full experience of the Self, then when looking back we will see that there is no wall. There has never been a wall. The wall is only in our imagination, which created a difference between the Self and everything else. Yet the Self is never absent from our experience, essential as it is to every experience of the inner and outer worlds. It is only so evident that it appears to be absent.

When truly looking from the point of view of the Self, we will see the Self in everything - including in our own little Ego. We will love everything - including our Ego. We will know our Ego as it is and we will know it will evolve, like a child growing up, until it merges with the Self. When truly connected inside, how can one reproach this child for being a child ?

So we will no longer be in any hurry. We will not dislike the current state of our Ego. We will just smile at it and try to guide it further on, without undue expectation, knowing this spiritual work can take many lifetimes. The ocean does not get disturbed by the waves on its surface and even an emotional tsunami is just a passing phase.

Suppose some people stay in a spiritual place for some days, where they do yoga, meditate, have nice people around, enjoy simple things like nature or chanting together. Then they start feeling very good, getting a taste of the bliss of the Self. When they go home, feeling refreshed and positive, maybe soon the feeling is lost. It is only natural that this happens, because there is usually less time for practice, more stress, and more interaction with people that have a more negative orientation. It hurts. Then people may have a tendency to start blaming themselves, to hate their sensitive Ego for its inability to keep the inner peace.

They might even somehow blame those they love, like their children or their partner, feeling that these are standing in the way of their spiritual progress. They may want to be free of all that, so that they can be this Buddha or yogi that they dream of. And then when reading more books or hearing teachings that advise to "just" destroy the Ego, people get frustrated. They start feeling stupid, inadequate, lose faith in themselves, become disillusioned. The very idea of the enlightened yogi becomes painful to them, when it should be a source of hope and inspiration.

So partially this negative attitude towards life and our Ego comes from peeking over the wall without climbing it. One is not to blame. To climb over the wall takes time. It's a process. Keep on peeking, keep on tasting. When life calls us back to our responsibilities, we accept it as our destiny, which no one can escape from. Keep on believing that there is something beyond the wall. And most of all, keep on believing that just like any yogi we will one day truly find ourselves on the other side. Then we will laugh at our struggle to jump over a non-existing wall, as much as we will laugh at any attempt to think that there is no wall while walking right into it.

After my first deep meditation I laughed for days. I couldn't take anything seriously. And I have never forgotten it. Since that time, I have encountered many problems, often lost my way, felt trapped even in persistent negative emotions, but never have I actually felt hopeless. Never have I truly hated my Ego, because since then, I know it for what it is. It is only a natural thing. And I know who I truly am. That Self which I am can never be lost, is never out of reach. However far away it feels, I can always go there, reconnect.

Progress takes time and in itself this path - though sometimes difficult - is truly beautiful and heroic. In its never ending attempt to be happy, whether by trying to meditate or by searching for a pretty flower, the Ego is just so beautiful. It carries many gifts and talents and tells a unique story each second of every day.

It is good to accept that, as long as we haven't moved beyond the wall, to do so remains a main desire. It is a very good desire to have, for ourselves and those around us. To honor this desire, we may have to detach from all other desires for a while[57]. We may need to spend some time, weeks, months, to pursue this desire.

We need to do this with a positive attitude, please, without hating everything else, without hating our other desires, without being dissatisfied with our Ego. We stop hating the mosquitoes that sting our nose as we try to meditate. We exclude any negative attitude towards anything that disturbs our meditation, our duties that take away our time for meditation, anything that takes away our attention.

It is fantastic to meditate where there are a lot of mosquitoes. If one can let them sting, become

---

[57] "Vayraga" in Sanskrit - detachment, see youtube.com/youyoga "Detached Attachment".

undisturbed by it, feeling no hatred for them, then the meditation will be fruitful. In meditation, our relationship to the mosquitoes and to our mind and Ego should be of the same kind. Nothing disturbs our meditation except us. First of all, we have to lose our impatience.

13

MOTIVATION

It is only natural for all practitioners to sometimes encounter issues with motivation and discipline, especially as we enter the third phase of the path towards enlightenment. If we cannot blame society and circumstances for our lack of effort and progress, we blame ourselves. Maybe for not practicing enough, for our addictions, for our lack of steady awareness.

We may feel that a negative attitude toward ourselves is not only justified, but also needed. We so much would like to jump up, rather than taking the stairs. We seek to inflate the problem in order to motivate ourselves to diligently work in finding a solution. This analysis of the issue of the Ego and its less yogic desires is based on a feeling of inferiority. So, it cannot strengthen our will power and motivation, quite the opposite. Unfortunately, many teachings also support the approach of forced motivation.

In trying to focus us on the goal of finding the Self,

some teachings totally reject the Ego. Yet the fact that humanity is so easily distracted, is no excuse for it. The Ego can appear as a demon for sure, but it also frequently shows itself as an angel. The Ego can be selfish, ugly, cruel, pitiful. Yet that potential for negativity also makes it truly beautiful, courageous, loving and funny, whenever it shows those positive qualities.

It is the Ego who has to decide to meditate, not the Self. The desire to destroy the Ego originates with the Ego and also needs the Ego in order to be fulfilled. The Ego is the true hero of yoga, even when performing the yoga of non-doing. A demonized, guilt-ridden Ego will forever stand in the way of truth, in the way of Self-realization, in the way of deep meditation. We need .faith in the power of yogic practices, in the beautiful process of spiritual growth. Impatience leads nowhere. To motivate ourselves so forcefully towards serious practice, in fact demotivates. We care for what we love and hurt what we hate.

The central purpose of yoga concerns the relationship between the Ego and the Self, which cannot be separated from the relationship between the Ego and the Ego. When we can't love ourselves, how can we love the Self, which is who we are ? How do we identify with a divine one that seems so totally different, alien to oneself ?

The misunderstanding is also caused by a lack of personalized teaching. The ancient teacher-student relationship was very direct and adapted the teachings to the individual. Disciplined practice would be measured to each individual's ability, willpower, experience, duties and desires. Nowadays most teachers don't have time for this kind of personal coaching. The more large and diverse the teacher's audience becomes, the more the teachings become generalized. Thus they can be easily misinterpreted and lack the compassion that every true teacher will express when communicating directly with the individual seeker. Then if an Ego issue needs to be addressed by the teacher, the Ego of the student will not feel attacked, but rather lovingly inspired towards making the wise choice.

Motivation depends on confidence and confidence depends on self-esteem. What kind of self-esteem can we have when believing that our Ego and our desires are very bad ? How will we feel if some day we fail to do the one hour of meditation that we have promised to do, which can happen to anybody ? And how hard will it be to believe that we can get rid of all desires forever ? Like weeds, they continuously prove the opposite by popping up again and again.

It is so much more motivating to see that, while setting aside other desires for a while is important to reach the Self, they don't need to be set aside forever. It is much more motivating to see our Ego as a natural phenomenon, whose evolution to a higher state of being is a natural process. Who wouldn't feel confident knowing that while this process can be facilitated by doing regular meditation and other disciplines, it cannot be forced. Accept, breath, focus, smile.

Then if one day we feel less up to it and our other desires are pressing hard for attention, we won't feel bad about it. In most cases we will be able to gather our strength and say "Just wait a while to let me do this one hour of meditation, then I can have some tea". And if somehow the one hour did not happen, the next day it will be so much easier to just pick up the practice again. That is because we have not attached to the error of yesterday. It has not degraded our Self-confidence, just win some lose some, you know. Having Self-confidence, we can be relaxed without getting lazy, focused without being tense, which is a subtle essential balance in all yoga practice.

One of the dangers in embracing a certain yoga tradition or technique, is that we tend to believe it is the only thing which is needed to reach our goal. The enthusiasm for our practice tends to create disdain towards all other practices, which is also an Ego game : my god is better than your god, my yoga is better than your yoga. Believing one is following the only right path can be seen as very motivating. Unfortunately, this common error is also a real danger to our motivation in the long run. Any particular practice works only on one particular part of us. The five main yogic paths exist to assure that we remove all blockages inside. Even if we all naturally develop personal preferences, sticking to only one of the paths guarantees one will get stuck somewhere. Thus the Ego loses the self-confidence that fundamental change is possible. The one who follows a path to a dead end, retraces his steps and continues walking.

No teaching should be that condescending as to tell us that our Ego is bad, that our desires are bad, that we are not good enough as we are. Even if they are inspired by the best intentions, they are misleading and robbing us of our energy and motivation. No yogic path or tradition can claim the title of best yoga for everyone. The best yoga is the one which works best for you. The objective of all paths in yoga is the same, yet the best way to reach this objective is different for everyone, because everyone starts from themselves. Just as the best road to New York depends on where we are heading from, the best yoga depends on who we are, as individuals.

14
A BUSINESS MODEL

The business interests of many spiritual teachers and organizations benefit from attacking the Ego and its desires. Likewise the marketing of their particular path is strengthened by positioning it as the best yoga for all. The more the students feel that they are in the dark, the more they are attracted to the light of the self-proclaimed enlightened teacher. The more they feel guilty about themselves, the more they are willing to offer selfless service to the organization and the higher the donations they are willing to make. The more these students are convinced that they are following the straightest path, the more they will pay for getting a map.

Religions tend to master this art to perfection and more so when they are in league with the leaders of a country. The best thing a leader can do to keep the people under control is to create a strong religious feeling of guilt, shame, worthlessness. We are taught to love everyone as our neighbor, yet excluding ourselves. Sure one can feel unworthy when faced with the divine, but that feeling is an illusion in the eye of the divine. One is never unworthy of progress.

Many people do many good things based on their religious feeling. Many religious people try very hard to bring positive change. Religions also successfully connect communities in common spiritual practices. Yet all too often religious traditions are used by people who have their own agenda in making people feel most unholy, unworthy, undeserving.

So, this negative attitude towards who we naturally are is also a matter of power and money, a form of mental oppression, a business marketing model, a political model. It preys on our occasional unhappiness, impatience and lack of motivation and discipline. There is no need to explain this any further - we have thousands of years of history to prove it.

15

NON-DUALITY

The mistake of unproductive Ego-bashing is not only found in religion and the more religious forms of yoga. It can also occur on the path of non-dual knowledge[58], the rational approach to yoga. Non-duality recognizes the Self as the ultimate truth beyond all dualities. Non-duality combines an intellectual change of perspective through non-dual understanding with a very simple but difficult technique of "just" observing or stopping thoughts. It represents the most basic yoga philosophy and is essentially non-religious and very popular these days because of this. Besides, who doesn't like the doctor who cures all with just one pill ?

Non-duality teaches that all the problems of the Ego and its desires can be solved by stopping all thought and thereby stopping all desires. And that is

---

[58] "Advaita Vedanta" in Sanskrit, associated with Jnana Yoga, see "The Yoga of Truth", Peter Marchand, Destiny Books 2007, ISBN-13 978-1-59477-165-1.

of course totally true, if one can do it. Whichever question the student has, the answer is always the same. Find out who is asking the question. Find out who is having the desires. Just mindfully witness thoughts and desires and they will magically melt away like snow in the sun of the Self. And again it is absolute truth, provided one can do it. Live only in the now, forget about yesterday, don't fantasize about tomorrow, don't postpone enlightenment, just be, just stop, be quiet.

I also teach this highly valuable technique[59], which always should come first and last. By first, I mean that many smaller desires and unhappy emotions can easily be rendered powerless by simply taking some distance, by stopping to take things personally, refraining from identification and taking the witnessing position. This technique of focus without object is also always last after the other techniques like breathing or mantra have been used. These should always be followed by some pure inner silence, some true holding still. Because of the calming power of those techniques, it will then be easier to be truly silent inside. And it will bring a lot.

But for most people, it will just not be enough. Not

---

[59] See youtube.com/youyoga "Jnana Yoga Technique".

even one in one thousand will hear this class and be able to durably stop thinking, identifying, desiring, trying. Any one of us can be among that small percentage of ready seekers at some point in our lives. For that precious moment, such teaching is not only valuable, but essential in not letting the opportunity go to waste. Yet, the rest of the time, most people require more, a lot more. Their Egos need to be taken a little more seriously, need a little more compassionate, workable advice, rather than just being told to shut up.

The danger in non-duality is that people get so enthusiastic about it that they tend to believe that all problems on the path can be solved by it. While this enthusiasm is understandable and in a way also a fruitful phase, many of these people even seem convinced that all our issues should be solved exclusively by non-duality. Non-duality has to include duality, otherwise how can it be non-dual? Disdainfully excluding all other yogic practices as Ego-centered nonsense, initial advancement is followed by frustration and a loss of common sense. Non-duality only directly affects our thinking and our ability to sense the existence of the Self, while we also have a body, deeper feelings, a reptile brain, a soul with quite a bit of luggage.

Obviously the famous original non-dual teachers like Ramana, Nisargadatta or Papaji[60] offer Self-knowledge as the ultimate direct answer to every problem people bring forward. They try to teach a difficult technique, so they prefer people to stick to it for a while, giving it a real chance. But if a student says he or she can't stop thinking even after trying very hard, they will also point towards other techniques, such as mantra meditation or breath control. And as Ramana would say, if even these do not work to calm down the mind, then one should first try to make life less stressful, take a holiday.

We should not get too side-tracked by such indirect techniques, so after the postures are done and the mantra is finished, it is advisable to return to the techniques that lead more directly to the Self. There is a lot of side tracking going on indeed and that is why the original non-dual teachers feel they don't need to teach mantra meditation and such. In India there are so many who do that. There is no condemnation of these techniques however, which are presented as having their place on the path of yoga. The Vedic tradition has a lot more to offer than non-dualism

---

[60] Ramana Maharishi, his student Papaji and also Nisargadatta Maharaj are great Jnana teachers who lived in the 20th Century.

alone. The traditional non-dual teachers know very well that for most people, the indirect techniques are a requirement to keep mind a little stable, to give the Ego a little more confidence and to make any true experience of the Self at all possible.

Non-duality does not demonize the Ego or its desires. At first, it certainly doesn't make us feel guilty about ourselves. Acceptance of all inner and outer experiences is key and that is very wise. Yet frustration is a certainty when the Ego and its desires are seen as a total distraction, which should not get any attention, should not be thought about. By believing that the solution is this simple, many are lead into unfruitful inner conflict, stagnation and guilt. As the solution is simple and not simple at the same time, oversimplifying it becomes quite complicated, especially for the Ego.

Sure the Ego can use some "bashing" sometimes and some people might just be ready to receive it. However this Ego-bashing should not become a fashion, nor the only "service" offered by the teachings. In the ancient way, the teacher takes full responsibility for the transformation of the student.

The internet also plays a role, because of the huge availability of spiritual information. I still remember paying lots of overweight charges when flying back from India, because of the many precious books I could buy nowhere else. With today's internet, the one who is willing to learn yoga philosophy can do so at an incredible speed, intellectually. Yet teachings need to be digested and put into practice to be properly understood. If one hears the same teacher say that mind needs to be controlled and needs to be ignored, what to believe? Only doing brings real understanding.

Changing our perspective is very important, but it is just a tiny first step. Thoughts don't count for much if our feeling is not behind it. The conscious mind plays only a minor role in the transformation of our Ego. The true seat of the Ego and our desires, frustrations and fears is in the subconscious mind. Our conscious mind is just a reflection of it and the only true progress, the only factual letting go, happens in our innermost subconscious soul. This requires more than just a non-dual change of mind, unless we want to keep thinking about not thinking, desiring not to desire.

16

THE DIVINE EGO

From the point of view of the divine, everything is divine. Not just by simply being part of the whole or because of the formless presence of the Self in everything. Every being also has a unique divine form potential, the divine Ego[61]. An apple tree does not need to grow mangoes. It can grow the greatest apples. It can manifest the divine form of the apple tree. That requires some identification with being an apple tree, some divine apple tree Ego. Key for this ultimate Ego is just to be, much like the Self just is.

The divine form of the Ego is the eternal beloved of the Self. From that unshakable love connection, the Ego emerges as a divine child so beautiful that it is the embodiment of life, art, romance and love. It has no doubts at all and is ever dancing in total union with the Self and in absolute harmony with everything. This

---

[61] "Radhe" in Sanskrit, the form of the divine Ego, ever in love with Krishna, the Self, see youtube.com/youyoga "Divine Energies of Hinduism".

divine actor is beyond enlightenment.

While we have described the seven steps towards enlightenment, we have not looked at what happens next. Where does all this yoga lead us ? When the purest energy and the purest consciousness become one without form, liberation follows[62]. Afterwards, manifestation is renewed, as the play of the three essential qualities of energy[63] again manifest, while consciousness remains entirely established in itself[64].

The one who thus becomes liberated[65] is truly free. Scripture describes how enlightened beings may then choose to dissolve in pure cosmic conscious energy or to manifest in any form. Enlightened being in manifested form means to live in a natural, unforced state of absorption in the Self[66]. This state is not different from what is found in deepest meditation. Yet instead of complete withdrawal from the universe, there is total inclusion of the universe. All is one.

Here our body, energy, conscious and

---

[62] Freely translated from the Patanjali Yoga Sutra 3.56.

[63] "The "Gunas" "Rajas, Tamas & Sattva" in Sanskrit – the essential qualities of energy, see youtube.com/youyoga "Yoga & Ayurveda".

[64] Freely translated from the Patanjali Yoga Sutra 4.34.

[65] "Kaivalya" in Sanskrit, the liberation preceding enlightenment or Moksha.

[66] "Sahaja Samadhi" in Sanskrit, see youtube.com/youyoga "Samadhi".

subconscious mind, as well as the Self are united by the divine form of the Ego. It's lotus blossom has roots deep into the mud, yet shines beautifully above the surface for all to enjoy. Consciousness descends from the crown chakra to the now fully open lotus of the heart[67], a subtle center within the heart chakra. True detached attachment is reached, which is not some detachment balanced with some attachment. It is full detachment in union with full attachment. Self and Ego are as one, without either losing its specific nature. They are two halves of the same one being. They are the two buckets that the yoke of yoga allows us to carry in balance[68].

A divine Ego is not a contradiction in terms. Anyhow, words fall short to describe such a state. Yet to just lift a hand, some identification is needed. It is quite irrelevant whether the divine Ego allows or orders body and mind to make it happen. As it is for the Self, the divine Ego can be simultaneously seen as empty and full. In this state, Self and divine Ego actually become quite indistinguishable.

---

[67] "Ananda Kanda" in Sanskrit, the spiritual heart, see youtube.com/youyoga "Desires of the Chakras".

[68] "Yoga" in Sanskrit literally means a yoke, a tool used to carry two weights on the shoulders.

One might say that this state is the summmum bonum[69] of the universe. However, before personally attaching to this idea of our supreme alter Ego, remember that it requires nothing less than enlightenment. For the rebirth of the holy Ego to happen, first the Ego has to die.

Contrary to popular belief, enlightenment is not necessarily a permanent state. All living saints who I have encountered as well as scripture[70], confirm that the enlightened one remains free to again lose that enlightened state. Liberation is absolute and does not sentence one to remain forever detached from everything. Much like the universe in the Vedic view is recreated over and over again from obviously enlightened conscious cosmic energy, the enlightened one may again and again enter the game of life and illusion[71]. There are numerous examples of Hindu deities even, who after incarnating, become

---

[69] Latin for the highest good or objective.

[70] As an example by excellence, see the "Yoga Vasistha" or "The Supreme Yoga" by Swami Venkatesananda, Motilal Banarsidas New Delhi 2005.

[71] "Leela and Maya" in Sanskrit, see youtube.com/youyoga "Leela, the Game of Self-Knowledge".

quite human in their emotional attachments[72].

So the truth is that as the Self, we are all already enlightened and that enlightenment is not necessarily an end point nor a permanent state. The enlightened being chooses to remain enlightened every second. And while the Ego needs to be destroyed to make enlightenment possible, it is only to rise from the ashes in its ultimate natural form.

In the space between our thoughts, we all have similar moments, seconds maybe, where we truly live from the heart. We all have some experience of being totally unconcerned, unforced, unattached. There that divine form of the Ego manifests. Its potential always lives inside us, along with the Self. A divinely brave, natural child precedes the frightened inner child that is the more commonly known Ego.

The natural, unforced state of absorption found in enlightened beings may also be somewhat approached by the state of divine artistic inspiration[73]. While the yogi seeks the divine, the true artist manifests it. When all doubt is dropped, the inner

---

[72] The god Ram for example, incarnation of Lord Vishnu, was overcome by grief and worry when his wife Sita, incarnation of the goddess Lakshmi, was abducted by a demon, see the famous Ramayan scripture.

[73] "Prathiba" in Sanskrit, see youtube.com/youyoga "The Sound of Silence".

.

muse is followed and one becomes totally absorbed in the music or the painting, magic happens. Whatever form the art takes, it makes the inherent imperfection of each form, perfect in its imperfection. When that supreme artist prays to the elements, they answer. We only have to allow it to happen.

It is the state of innocent confidence that we sometimes can see in children, in wild animals or in the natural pride of people from original cultures that live close to nature. As men or women, as fathers or sisters, as teachers or taxi drivers, as martial artists, carpenters or computer programmers, we can just be what we are doing in the moment. Each role complements the other. Thus we dance the eternal dance of mirroring our dance partners[74]. We are listening, we chose to follow and yet are not without inherent direction ourselves. We all have our moments when our Ego touches the heavens. And we all have our rather stupid, deluded moments. Acceptance of nature is key in both cases.

---

[74] "Tandava & Lasya" in Sanskrit, performed by Shiva and Parvati, see youtube.com/youyoga "Divine Energies of Hinduism".

.

17
ONE LOVE

Our Ego has been looking at length into the mirror. It can be trouble or bliss. The only one who causes trouble about the Ego is the Ego. Trouble comes from trouble. Bliss comes from bliss. It is Ego's job to decide which is which. Some chai on the way is not that bad.

Condemning the Ego is asking for trouble. Loving the Ego is bliss. The process to transform the Ego will take quite a while, even if we want it to be fast. We are free to take our natural time. A work in progress is timeless, unhurried. In any undertaking, self-confidence is the key. Any hurry belongs to the troubled Ego. Why not simultaneously accept our imperfection as well as our eternal opportunity for growth towards perfection ? Let us just solve this little riddle and then enlightenment can wait, cause we will be quite alright, already.

If we can accept that the Ego and the Self exist simultaneously, then we are at least halfway there. Do not separate them, bring them together where they are and belong. Be the Self and be yourself, that's it. And if from that state of union, we want to do something, there is no need to hold back. Manifest the divine.

We are all children, growing quite indefinitely. We do not need to be perfect. We are the art of life, the purpose of creation. We are the knower, the knowing and the known. We grow into whomever we want to be. Everyone has an Ego and every Ego has a purpose, a script, an ultimate form. Each second counts as an eternity, an absolutely unique step in the universal dance.

The Self loves our Ego as itself, sees no difference. How can we live from the Self if we can't accept the Ego as it does ? Love starts from love. Love yourself unconditionally. Accept the Self and in doing so accept yourself as you are. Connect heaven and earth. Live with the entirety of your Being. Do not divide, unite. Be like an arrow shot from the heart.

Love your Ego as you love your Self. One love.

ABOUT THE AUTHOR

Peter Marchand teaches Jnana, Karma, Bhakti, Ashtanga and Tantra Yoga. As a personal coach, he guides people from around the world towards happiness, inner peace and deeper meditation. He is also a Tantric healer, following an ancient Nepalese shamanic tradition. Originally inspired by his teacher Harish Johari, Peter is one of the founders of Sanatan Society. As the author also of "The Yoga of the Nine Emotions" and "The Yoga of Truth", he lives in Belgium.

Contact Peter through
www.leela-yoga.org
for personal coaching
and healing through
video calls and visits.

Thank you for posting your feedback
on this book at Amazon & at
facebook.com/peter.marchand.71

Made in the USA
San Bernardino, CA
11 November 2019

59719928R00056